DATE DUE		

Peace Corps

Celeste A. Peters

WEIGL PUBLISHERS INC.

Dedication

This series is dedicated to those people who help make their community, state, and world a better place. Volunteering is one way to become an active and responsible citizen. The thoughtfulness and hard work of volunteers is an inspiration to all. International Organizations is both an acknowledgment of and a tribute to volunteers.

Credits

Project Coordinator
Michael Lowry
Copy Editor
Heather Kissock
Photo Researcher
Gayle Murdoff
Design and Layout
Warren Clark
Bryan Pezzi

Published by Weigl Publishers Inc.
123 South Broad Street, Box 227
Mankato, MN 56002
USA

Web site: www.weigl.com
Copyright ©2003 WEIGL PUBLISHERS INC.

Library of Congress Cataloging-in-Publication Data

Peters, Celeste.
  Peace Corps / Celeste Peters.
    v. cm. -- (International organizations)
Includes index.
Contents: An organization is born -- The mission -- Key issues -- International organizations -- U.S. operations -- Achievements -- Current initiatives -- Take action!
  ISBN 1-59036-023-0
  1. Peace Corps (U.S.)--Juvenile literature.
[1. Peace Corps (U.S.)]
I. Title. II. Series.
  HC60.5 .P49 2002
  361.6--dc21
                                          2002006565

Printed in Canada
1 2 3 4 5 6 7 8 9 0   06 05 04 03 02

Photo Credits

Contents

What is the Peace Corps? 4
An Organization is Born 6
The Mission 8
Key Issues 10
Around the World 16
U.S. Operations 18
Milestones 20
Current Initiatives 24
Take Action! 28
In the Classroom 30
Further Reading/Web Sites 31
Glossary/Index 32

What is the Peace Corps?

The Peace Corps is an organization of volunteers from the United States that promotes world peace and friendship. Members of the Peace Corps live and work in a **developing country** for two years. While there, they share their skills and knowledge with the country's citizens.

By forming relationships with people from around the world, Peace Corps volunteers create a better understanding of Americans. At the same time, the volunteers learn about their host country. They learn the people's traditions and cultures. When the volunteers return to the United States, they share this information with other Americans. In this way, the Peace Corps provides Americans with a better understanding of other cultures.

Peace Corps workers are called volunteers because they do not work for money. Instead, they gain valuable life skills while they are away. Many learn foreign languages and important career skills. Peace Corps volunteers return to the United States richly rewarded by the personal satisfaction of helping others.

While abroad, Peace Corps members volunteer their time in a variety of areas. They teach English and many other subjects. They work with communities to protect the environment and gain access to clean water. Volunteers help families grow more food and stay healthy. Some members also help people who wish to start small businesses. The main goal of Peace Corps volunteers is to help people take control of their own futures.

> "To those people … across the globe struggling to break the bonds of mass misery, we pledge our best efforts to help them help themselves."
>
> **President John F. Kennedy**

The average age of Peace Corps volunteers is 28 years old.

Quick Fact

To serve in the Peace Corps, you must be an American citizen who is at least 18 years old. Most volunteers have university degrees.

Just the Facts

Founded: The Peace Corps was created on March 1, 1961.

Founders: In the late 1950s, Congresspeople Henry Reuss and Hubert Humphrey came up with the idea of the Peace Corps. John F. Kennedy supported the idea and officially created the Peace Corps. In 1961, R. Sargent Shriver was appointed the first director of the Peace Corps.

Mission: To promote world peace and friendship by helping people in developing countries help themselves.

Total volunteers and trainees since 1961: 165,000

Current volunteers and trainees: 7,000

Number of countries served since 1961: 135

Scope of work: Agriculture, business and community development, education, environment, and health

An Organization is Born

On the night of October 14, 1960, John F. Kennedy asked 10,000 University of Michigan students if they would be prepared to promote world peace by volunteering in a foreign country. At the time, Kennedy was running for the presidency of the United States. The campaign speech he made that night began the Peace Corps movement.

At the time, the United States and the Soviet Union were engaged in a **cold war**. People around the world feared the possibility of war. However, Kennedy was interested in promoting peace. He told the students that he wanted to form an organization of young people who would help the world become a better place to live.

The students were impressed and, within a few days, the movement was underway. More than 1,000 students signed a petition of support. Two of the students, Alan and Judy Guskin, gave the petition to Kennedy. This list convinced him that Americans shared his dream.

Kennedy became the thirty-fifth president of the United States on January 20, 1961. Immediately, he began work on the creation of a Peace Corps.

> " ... My fellow citizens of the world: ask not what America will do for you, but what together we can do for the freedom of man."
> **President John F. Kennedy**

On March 1, 1961, President John F. Kennedy signed the executive order that founded the Peace Corps.

PROFILE

R. Sargent Shriver

The job of setting up the Peace Corps fell to R. Sargent Shriver, its first director. The day after he became president, Kennedy asked Shriver to "report how the Peace Corps should be organized and then to organize it." Kennedy also wanted the report done within one month.

Shriver was born in Westminster, Maryland, on November 9, 1915. He studied at Yale Law School and served as a naval officer during World War II. After the war, he met Kennedy's father, Joseph. Joseph Kennedy was impressed by Shriver's drive and hired him to run a large store that he owned in Chicago. Shriver later married Joseph's daughter, Eunice. The marriage made John F. Kennedy and Shriver brothers-in-law.

"Peace must become the world's number one objective."
R. Sargent Shriver

Shriver would remain director of the Peace Corps until 1966. At first, the nation saw the program as an experiment. Some people thought that the Peace Corps should start with only a few projects and volunteers.

Shriver thought differently. He later wrote, "We knew the Peace Corps would have only one chance to work. As with the parachute jumper, the chute had to open the first time."

In a short period, Shriver set up projects in fifty-five countries. When he left the Peace Corps, more than 14,500 volunteers were serving overseas.

Shriver's next job was head of the United States War on Poverty program. From 1968 to 1970, he served as the United States ambassador to France. Shriver even ran for the position of vice president in 1972, but lost. Today, a conference room in the Peace Corps building is named Shriver Hall.

The Mission

The Peace Corps began as an experiment. No one knew if it would work. Would developing countries ask the Peace Corps for help? Would young people actually apply to join and serve? Would the Peace Corps be capable of achieving its mission of promoting peace by "helping others help themselves"? Many questions were left unanswered.

> " … I made a difference in their lives, and I'm really proud of that."
>
> **Azikiwe Chandler, Peace Corps Volunteer**

Today, we know that the Peace Corps was and is a success. It has been operating for more than forty years. During that time, 135 countries have asked for help. More than 165,000 volunteers have gone overseas to assist. Some work with **at-risk youth**. Others help build schools or dig wells for clean water. There is no lack of work to be done.

Peace Corps volunteers serve in five main regions of the world:
- Africa
- Central America and the Caribbean
- Central and East Asia,
- Europe and the Mediterranean
- the Pacific

During the early years of the Peace Corps, volunteers mainly taught in schools, helped farmers grow more food, and showed people how to gain access to clean water. Today, volunteer work has branched out into other areas.

For instance, **AIDS** has killed millions of Africans. Millions more are sick and will soon die. Peace Corps volunteers in Africa now teach people how to stop the spread of AIDS.

As well, hurricanes and earthquakes often strike Central America and the Caribbean. When they hit, they destroy homes and food supplies. Peace Corps volunteers are helping the people there find ways to build safer homes and protect their food crops from hurricane and earthquake damage.

A great deal of change is taking place in some countries in Asia, Eastern Europe, and the Mediterranean. For the first time, people in these countries are permitted to own their own businesses. Peace Corps volunteers are helping them start companies and learn business skills. These skills include how to use computers.

Volunteers in the Pacific region are working to educate young people. Many of these youth have a difficult time finding and keeping jobs. Some are tempted to turn to a life of crime. Peace Corps volunteers help these youths find meaningful responsibilities within the community instead.

More than 60 percent of Peace Corps volunteers are female.

The three goals of the Peace Corps are:

- to help the people of interested countries meet their need for trained men and women

- to help the people in these countries better understand Americans

- to help Americans better understand the people of other countries

Key Issues

Education

Education has always been an important focus of the Peace Corps. People from other countries learn valuable skills from Peace Corps workers. At the same time, Americans learn about other cultures. It is a two-way exchange of information.

Some Peace Corps workers have studied to become teachers. These volunteers specialize in education. Many of them give classes in English, math, and science. These workers also help local teachers improve their teaching skills. Sometimes education volunteers help build schools and libraries. If needed, they also help find books.

> "The kids I taught were always with me ... I always wanted to have children, but I never thought I'd have so many and so soon."
>
> **Tina Martin, Peace Corps Volunteer**

In other countries, not everyone is lucky enough to go to school. Often, education volunteers work with adults who have never learned to read. In some areas of the world, only boys go to school. In these communities, volunteers help women and girls obtain an education, too.

One of the most important things that education volunteers do is show people how to deal with everyday problems. They work with local teachers to create lessons that are based on problems that the community is facing. For example, many people in a village might be getting sick. In this case, a Peace Corps volunteer could help prepare lessons on how to avoid catching diseases. The students might learn about germs or how to **sterilize** water. They would learn science that applies to their lives.

Quick Fact •

In many African countries, less than half of the girls between the ages of 6 and 11 go to school.

CASE STUDY
Kimberly Susan Ross

Kimberly Ross is a Peace Corps education volunteer who teaches English in Guinea, West Africa. She lives in a mud hut in the village of Kouroussa.

Kimberly has noticed that more and more people in Guinea want to speak English. She tutors many students and adults in her home. Kimberly says that English is becoming more important to the people in Guinea. They think of it as the business language of the world. Also, many English-speaking people are moving to Guinea from neighboring countries. These people are trying to escape from wars in their homelands. The Guineans would like to be able to talk with them.

"I teach English to four different classes, a total of twenty hours a week. Two of my classes have only ten to twelve students, but the other two have forty-five to sixty kids. No students in Guinea have dictionaries or English textbooks. They must spend half of each class copying words, grammar rules, and text that I write on the blackboard. On special days we play Simon Says, practice tongue twisters, or translate American songs."
Kimberley Susan Ross

Health

Millions of people in developing countries become sick every year from drinking polluted water. Many even die. Peace Corps health volunteers help people in these countries stay healthy. They teach them how to stay clean and how to choose and cook nutritious foods. Sometimes volunteers help communities obtain safe drinking water. They dig new wells for fresh water. They also build **latrines** and show the local people how to keep them working properly.

Not all diseases come from polluted water. Some sicknesses, like colds or AIDS, pass from person to person. Other diseases pass from animals to humans. Malaria, for example, passes from mosquitoes to humans. Still other diseases, such as lung cancer, can be due to things people choose to do, like smoking. Health volunteers teach people ways to lessen their chances of catching these illnesses.

Each community has its own set of health problems. The Peace Corps' main focus is to help the people in the community learn to take care of themselves.

Africa was the first place that Peace Corps volunteers went to in 1961. Since then, more than 61,000 volunteers have served in Africa.

CASE STUDY
Elvis

Elvis is an 11-year-old orphan who has AIDS. He and eighty-five other children go to an orphan drop-in center in central Zimbabwe. Jessica Crary, a Peace Corps volunteer, works at the center and describes Elvis's struggle:

"Elvis first came to the center for lunch. The center paid for his school fees, helped him with homework, and dressed his sores daily. One day I was sitting with him and asked him to smile because he never did. He told me that he couldn't because he was in so much pain. I was devastated—what about his medications?

I asked Kuda, who was administering his medication.

She told me that Elvis's older brother had stolen the pain tablets, so Elvis wasn't even getting the medication. She told me Elvis stays in a brick house with his 15- and 18-year-old brothers. The tablet-stealing 21-year-old brother stays in a different part of town. The three boys sleep with three blankets on the floor. There is no food or source of income in the house.

We decided that Elvis would come to the center on the weekends for food. Without fail, Kuda would ensure that he was being fed and taking his medication. The sores on Elvis's body began to heal, and he slowly began smiling and talking more.

Today, Elvis is a different person. He runs and plays and laughs and talks and gets on well with the other children. It's an amazing thing to see."

Only about 40 percent of people living in the developing world have access to a safe and easily accessible water source.

Agriculture and Environment

It takes special skills to become a good farmer. Peace Corps agriculture volunteers help people overseas improve their farming skills. They also show them how to farm without damaging the environment.

Humans around the world grow crops and raise livestock. People feed themselves and their families with the food they grow. They also sell food to obtain money. In some parts of the world, though, farmers are unable to grow enough food to feed even their families.

Sometimes the soil is poor because the land has been farmed too much. In other cases, care has not been taken to protect the soil. Wind has blown the soil away, or water has carried it off. The ground that remains does not contain the nutrients that crops need to survive. Without crops, there are sometimes not enough plants in the area to feed livestock.

Peace Corps volunteers work with farmers on projects that meet the needs of the local community. They show farmers how to make the soil fertile again and how to prevent future erosion. In some places, volunteers help plant and grow vegetable gardens and fruit orchards. This is especially useful where children suffer from **malnutrition**. Fruits and vegetables contain vitamins and minerals that are important for good health.

While working with local farmers, volunteers also demonstrate ways to protect the environment. They show farmers how to reduce the use of harmful **pesticides** on crops. To preserve forests, they help the community find sources of fuel other than wood. Volunteers also work on recycling projects and projects that protect wildlife.

Some Peace Corps workers serve in communities where farming already supplies all of the food the people need to survive. In this case, the volunteers help find better ways to market and sell any extra food.

Quick Fact •

In most developing countries, 85 percent of the people work as farmers.

CASE STUDY
Lanette Woo

Lanette Woo served as a Peace Corps volunteer from 1995 to 1997. In 1991, she graduated from the University of California with a degree in **landscape architecture**. After working for a landscape design company for several years, Lanette became interested in gaining work experience overseas. After a friend told her about the Peace Corps, she decided to volunteer.

Lanette was interested in forestry. She wanted to go to the part of the world where the greatest amount of rain forest was being destroyed. Lanette applied to go to southeast Asia and was sent to Thailand.

While forestry was Lanette's main assignment, she did many other things as well. Lanette helped raise silkworms. She designed and helped build a pet nursery. She even ran a scholarship program for local high school girls.

When Lanette returned to the United States, she changed career paths and earned a master's degree in business administration. While pursuing this degree, Lanette used her Peace Corps experience to help small companies raise money.

"When I came home … I was able to build on my Peace Corps work in Thailand, helping people try to improve their operations and efficiency. Now I'm working for the Internet Services Group."
Lanette Woo

Around the World

The number of countries in which volunteers serve has steadily grown since the Peace Corps began operating in 1961. The first volunteers worked in one of two countries, Ghana or Tanzania. Today, the Peace Corps operates projects in 135 countries, and that number is still growing. Education projects are the most widespread. About one-third of the countries served by the Peace Corps host education projects.

Countries which have hosted Peace Corps volunteers are colored in yellow on this map.

THE CARIBBEAN
The Caribbean Basin Initiative is established in 1982.

CENTRAL AMERICA
In 1982, the Peace Corps launches the Initiative for Central America.

HUNGARY/POLAND
In 1990, Hungary and Poland become the first Eastern European countries to host Peace Corps workers.

ESTONIA/LATVIA/LITHUANIA
Peace Corps volunteers arrive in the former Soviet Union for the first time in 1992. They work on small business projects.

CHINA
China opens its doors to Peace Corps volunteers in 1993.

GHANA
In 1961, Ghana becomes the first country to receive Peace Corps volunteers.

GUINEA
The Crisis Corps is founded in 1995. One of the first countries to receive assistance is Guinea.

JORDAN
Jordan receives its first group of Peace Corps volunteers in 1997.

SOUTH AFRICA
The first group of Peace Corps volunteers to serve in South Africa arrive in 1997.

U.S. Operations

When Peace Corps volunteers come back to the United States, they often give talks and write about the people they met and the places they lived overseas.

The Peace Corps runs three programs in the United States. Two are school programs. The third matches donors with projects.

> "It is not uncommon to see Peace Corps volunteers digging wells or wielding a laptop."
>
> **Queen Noor of Jordan**

Peace Corps Fellows/USA

Some volunteers go back to university for a master's degree when they return home. If they agree to work in an **underserved community** at the same time, a special Peace Corps initiative, called the Fellows program, helps them pay for their education.

World Wise Schools

Peace Corps Director Paul D. Coverdell began the World Wise Schools program in 1989. The program connects students with currently serving Peace Corps volunteers all around the world. The goal is to bring cross-cultural understanding into the classroom.

Partnership Program

The Peace Corps Partnership Program lets Americans join the fight against poverty worldwide. The program links communities in need with individuals or groups in the United States who want to help by raising money. For example, a church group might collect money to help buy blankets for an orphanage in Thailand. The initiatives are planned by the people who live in the villages where Peace Corps volunteers work. These villagers must pay for at least 25 percent of the project themselves.

Quick Fact

Most volunteers are required to have a university degree to serve in the Peace Corps. Youth development volunteers and construction volunteers can have work experience instead.

CASE STUDY
Dorothy Sales

The Soviet Union, a large and powerful country, broke apart in 1994. The major regions of the former Soviet Union became independent countries. Dorothy Sales, a Peace Corps volunteer, went to one of these countries. From 1995 to 1997, Dorothy taught business courses in the Ukraine. She also set up a new center to help students find jobs after graduation.

When Dorothy arrived, the country was in the middle of writing a new **constitution**. It was also creating its own form of money and opening its first stock market. "To witness the foundation of an economy being built and to be a small part of it is an experience few will ever have, and one that was not lost on me. Each day, I found myself learning nearly as much as my students. I shared the excitement and eagerness in the classroom as students embraced the spirit of free enterprise. They wanted to learn how **free markets** work and how to compete within them, both at home and abroad. They worked hard to provide themselves with a framework for a better job, a better way of life."

"In some ways, the job was very similar to working in America. I dressed much like I did back in Boston and used my laptop at home to prepare for the next day's class. But there were exciting changes going on that made it much different."
Dorothy Sales

In 1992, the Ukraine requested business volunteers from the Peace Corps. Since then, more than 640 volunteers have served in the Ukraine.

Milestones

The Peace Corps has been helping people throughout the world for more than forty years. The Peace Corps teaches them how to stay healthy, grow food, and run small businesses.

1960s: Peace, Not War

The United States and the Soviet Union are not getting along with one another. Everyone is worried that a war will begin. The United States decides to do something that will help them develop friends around the world, not enemies. President John F. Kennedy creates the Peace Corps. R. Sargent Shriver is the organization's first director.

1950s

Congresspeople Henry Reuss and Hubert Humphrey propose the formation of organizations similar to the future Peace Corps. Reuss calls his organization the Point Four Youth Corps.

1960

When John F. Kennedy defeats Humphrey for the presidential nomination, Humphrey hands all of his research on the Peace Corps over to Kennedy.

1960

Henry Reuss introduces to the House of Representatives the first legislation that relates to the formation of a Peace Corps.

1960

John F. Kennedy asks 10,000 students at the University of Michigan if they would consider volunteering overseas. The students respond by collecting signatures of those interested in the formation of a Peace Corps. Their response convinces Kennedy of the need for such an organization.

1961

Less than two months after he becomes president, Kennedy signs an executive order that establishes the Peace Corps.

1961

President Kennedy holds a ceremony at the White House Rose Garden to honor the first Peace Corps volunteers.

1961

The first members of the Peace Corps go overseas. The fifty-one volunteers serve in Ghana and Tanzania. When the volunteers land in Ghana, they stand together and sing the Ghanaian national anthem in the local language, Twi.

1970s: Focus on Skills

The Peace Corps includes more men and women with professional skills than ever before. Doctors, engineers, and farming experts teach their skills to people in host countries. These people then share the new skills with others in their community. In this way, the gift of knowledge grows.

1974

A former Peace Corps volunteer, Chris Dodd, is elected to the House of Representatives.

1974

The number of countries served by the Peace Corps grows to sixty-nine.

1978

Paul Tsongas, a former Peace Corps volunteer, is elected to the United States Senate.

1979

President Jimmy Carter gives the Peace Corps the right to run on its own, separate from ACTION.

1963

The number of Peace Corps volunteers grows to 7,300 people working in forty-four countries.

1964

The Peace Corps Partnership Project begins in April. This program lets people at home become involved with overseas projects.

1965

Volunteers that have returned home hold their first conference.

1966

More than 15,000 men and women serve abroad. This is the greatest number of Peace Corps volunteers in the organization's history.

1971

President Richard Nixon's government creates a new federal volunteer agency called ACTION. This agency includes the Peace Corps, along with several other federal volunteer organizations.

1981

The U.S. Congress makes the Peace Corps an independent federal agency.

1981

The Peace Corps celebrates its twentieth anniversary.

1981

More than 97,000 volunteers have served in the Peace Corps to date.

1982

The Peace Corps' new Competitive Enterprise Development Program begins promoting the development of small businesses in host countries. Other new programs include the Caribbean Basin Initiative, the Initiative for Central America, and the African Food Systems Initiative.

1985

The Peace Corps Fellows Program begins at Columbia University. It prepares volunteers for service overseas and helps them get teaching jobs once they return to the United States.

1980s: New Programs

During the 1980s, the Peace Corps begins new programs, both overseas and at home. A great number of volunteers have already served overseas and are now back in the United States. They want to share their knowledge of other countries and cultures with their fellow Americans. Programs begin in grade schools and universities that call on this knowledge.

1990s: New Beginnings

In the early 1990s, the once powerful Soviet Union breaks up into smaller countries. The people in many of these countries want to start their own businesses. There is one large problem. The old Soviet Union did not allow people to run private companies. The people lack the skills they need to start their own businesses, so the Peace Corps begins training them. For the first time, volunteers also serve in Eastern Europe, China, South Africa, Jordan, Bangladesh, and Mozambique.

1986

The Peace Corps' twenty-fifth anniversary is celebrated in Washington, DC by 5,000 volunteers who have served overseas. The organization gives its archives to the John F. Kennedy Library.

1989

A new Peace Corps program called World Wise Schools lets students in more than 550 schools correspond with overseas volunteers.

1993

For the first time, a returned Peace Corps volunteer is appointed director of the organization. Carol Bellamy is the thirteenth director.

Peace Corps

2000s: More Friends

Terrorists attack the United States on September 11, 2001. As a result, the role of the Peace Corps becomes even more important than it was before. Americans feel that they and people from other cultures need to know one another much better. The number of Peace Corps volunteers grows.

1998

The Peace Corps moves into its own building in Washington, DC. Volunteers aid victims of hurricanes in Central America.

1999

Crisis Corps volunteers work with the World Food Program and CARE in northern Zambia, assisting refugees from the Democratic Republic of Congo.

2000

Volunteers begin helping communities in Venezuela that are damaged by heavy flooding.

2001

The Crisis Corps responds after two earthquakes hit Japan. Volunteers also help small businesses develop in war-torn Bosnia.

2002

President George W. Bush says he wants to double the number of Peace Corps volunteers. Within 24 hours, more than 500 Americans apply to join the Peace Corps on the Internet.

1995

Returned Peace Corps volunteers begin serving in the newly formed Crisis Corps. This program provides short-term help to victims of natural disasters and other crises.

1996

In April, the Peace Corps hosts the first Conference on International Volunteerism. In September, it launches the Loret Miller Ruppe Memorial Lecture Series.

1997

The Crisis Corps begins working in Guinea, a country in West Africa.

Current Initiatives

Expanded Services

On September 11, 2001, terrorists attacked the United States. They destroyed the World Trade Center in New York and badly damaged the Pentagon in Washington, D.C. Thousands died. Americans wondered why there was such hatred toward the United States. It became clear that Americans and the rest of the world needed to get to know one another better, and the Peace Corps could help.

In January 2002, President George W. Bush told the nation that he wanted to double the number of Peace Corps volunteers over the next five years. Some of these volunteers will serve in Afghanistan, where

> "The tremendous response of Americans who want to serve overseas with the Peace Corps is an inspiration."
> Lloyd Pierson, Peace Corps Acting Deputy Director

many years of war have left millions of people homeless. Other volunteers may go to Peru or East Timor. Both of these countries have recently invited the Peace Corps to send volunteers.

The Crisis Corps

Survivors of natural disasters or wars have a crisis on their hands. They need help in a hurry. That is why the Peace Corps has created a branch of its service called the Crisis Corps. The Crisis Corps is made up of volunteers who have served in the Peace Corps before. They have a great deal of experience and do not need to be trained. This makes them perfect for sudden or short-term assignments. Crisis Corps workers also help out when the Peace Corps needs extra hands. This is currently the case in Africa, where the Peace Corps is helping to fight the spread of AIDS.

Quick Fact ·

Crisis Corps assignments are usually three to six months in length.

CASE STUDY
Corcoran High School, Syracuse, New York

The students of Corcoran High School fund a Peace Corps Partnership Project every year. They have been doing this since 1983. The students raise money by selling cards that they draw. They also sell T-shirts that have peace as their theme.

> "Just because there are separate borders doesn't mean there have to be separate people."
> Jim Miller,
> Global Studies Teacher,
> Corcoran High School

So far, the high school students have donated more than $25,000 to Peace Corps projects. Their money has helped build five elementary schools. It has also helped build the very first school for the blind in central Africa. Recently, the school funded a reading project in Nigeria that was led by a volunteer who had graduated from Corcoran High School.

The students do more than raise money for each project. They also become pen pals with the villagers. They send letters and photos back and forth. Sometimes they even exchange small objects of interest. This lets the students get to know people and cultures around the world.

The Corcoran High School students share what they learn with younger students at nearby Roberts Elementary School. They teach the younger students dances, cooking, songs, and games from other countries. The younger students also help out with the Peace Corps projects. They collect pennies to buy small things the villages need, such as books or soccer balls.

AIDS Prevention in Africa

The deadly disease AIDS occurs worldwide. It kills more than 3 million people every year. Most of these people live in Africa. To date, more than 22 million Africans have caught the infection that causes AIDS, and more than 14 million Africans have died from the disease. Since most of the people who die from AIDS are adults, millions of children in Africa have been orphaned. Some of these children have the disease, too. This need not be the case because AIDS is preventable.

Many people in Africa catch AIDS because they do not know it exists. Others catch it because they do not know how it is passed along from one person to another. They do not know how to protect themselves.

Teaching people about AIDS is the best way to stop it from spreading. In 2000, the Peace Corps decided to step in and help. All volunteers serving in Africa are now trained to educate others about AIDS in the villages where they work.

Sharing Technology

In some parts of the world, people do not have enough money to buy a computer or the skills to use one. Most people in developing countries have never used a computer. They are being left behind as computers help the rest of the world move forward. The Peace Corps has decided to help them catch up.

The Peace Corps believes in sharing technology and knowledge. Almost all Peace Corps volunteers know how to use a computer and the Internet. They are now teaching these skills to the local businesses and young people they work with.

In some cases, the Peace Corps is also supplying computers or computer services. One volunteer in Guatemala has made a Web site for a group of Mayan women. They use it to sell the cloth they weave.

Quick Fact ·

In some African countries, one out of every four people between the ages of 15 and 49 years has AIDS.

CASE STUDY
Bob Findlay

Bob Findlay is a teacher at the University of Iowa who has a very valuable skill. He puts together plans that help communities prevent or respond to disasters. Bob first served in the Peace Corps when he worked in Colombia, South America, from 1963 to 1965. Since then, he has served in the Crisis Corps several times.

Recently, Bob went to Central America. He was looking for reasons to explain why hurricanes cause so much damage when they hit the coast of El Salvador. Bob immediately saw several problems. The local environment had been badly damaged. People had cut down too many trees. They had also built too many channels for bringing water from nearby rivers to their fields. These two factors allowed floodwaters to carry away good soil. Sometimes, the waters also carried away buildings and people. Bob noted that cities had spread out into these dangerous areas.

Once he identified these factors, Bob wrote a report. He showed the people of El Salvador where the problems were. The report also showed them how best to respond next time a hurricane came their way. Bob faced a large challenge when preparing the report because he had to remember how to write in Spanish.

Hurricane Gilbert was the strongest hurricane to hit the Western Hemisphere in the twentieth century. It struck in 1988 and devastated Jamaica and parts of Mexico. Winds gusted up to 218 miles per hour. Peace Corps volunteers are working to lessen the damage caused by hurricanes.

Take Action!

Become an active and responsible citizen by taking action in your community. Participating in local projects can have far-reaching results. You do not have to go overseas to get involved. You can do service projects like the ones the Peace Corps volunteers do no matter where you live. In fact, young people are helping out every day. Some help support overseas projects. Others volunteer for service projects in their home communities. Here are some examples:

"My friends and I organized a bottle drive at our school. Monthly we make maybe 100-something dollars. We donate our money to schools around the world that are in need of books, teachers … "

Leah from Northampton, MA

"I give my old clothes to the needy."

Todd from Chicago, IL

"I volunteered at the animal shelter during the summer. I walked dogs and cleaned kennels."

Anika from Hailey, ID

"I own a small little motorboat, and I live on a lake. Every once in a while during the summer, my friends and I go into the boat and drive around looking for trash and bad things in the lake."

Zack from Littleton, MA

"This summer I went to a camp in Maine. We did car washes to raise money to be sent to Nicaragua."

Laurel from Charlotte, VT

Where to Write

There are eleven Peace Corps offices across the United States. Write to the office nearest you.

Peace Corps Atlanta
100 Alabama Street
Building 1924
Suite 2R70
Atlanta, GA 30303

Peace Corps Boston
10 Causeway Street
Room 450
Boston, MA 02222

Peace Corps Chicago
55 West Monroe Street
Suite 450
Chicago, IL 60603

Peace Corps Dallas
207 South Houston St.
Room 527
Dallas, TX 75202

Peace Corps Denver
1999 Broadway
Suite 2205
Denver, CO 80202

**Peace Corps
Los Angeles**
11000 Wilshire Blvd.
Suite 8104
Los Angeles, CA 90024

**Peace Corps
Minneapolis**
330 Second Avenue
South Suite 420
Minneapolis, MN 55401

Peace Corps New York
201 N. Varick Street
Suite 1025
New York, NY 10014

**Peace Corps
San Francisco**
333 Market Street
Suite 600
San Francisco
CA 94105

Peace Corps Seattle
2001 Sixth Avenue
Suite 1776
Seattle, WA 98121

**Peace Corps
Washington, DC**
1525 Wilson Blvd.
Suite 250
Arlington, VA 22209

In the Classroom

EXERCISE ONE:

Make Your Own Brochure

Organizations such as the Peace Corps use brochures to inform the public about their activities. To make your own Peace Corps brochure, you will need:

- paper
- ruler
- pencil
- color pens or markers

1. Using your ruler as a guide, fold a piece of paper into three equal parts. Your brochure should now have a cover page, a back page, and inside pages.
2. Using your color markers, design a cover page for your brochure. Make sure to include a title.
3. Divide the inside pages into sections. Use the following questions as a guide.
    - What is the organization?
    - How did it get started?
    - Who started it?
    - Who does it help?
4. Using the information found in this book, summarize in point form the key ideas for each topic. Add photographs or illustrations.
5. On the back page, write down the address and contact information for the local Peace Corps office.
6. Photocopy your brochure, and give copies to your friends, family, and classmates.

EXERCISE TWO:

Send a Letter to Your Congressperson

To express concern about a particular issue, you can write a letter to your member of congress. This can be an effective way to make the government aware of issues that need its attention. To write a letter, all you need is a pen and paper or a computer.

1. Find out the name and address of your congressperson by contacting your local librarian. You can also search the Internet.
2. Write your name, address, and phone number at the top of the letter.
3. When addressing your letter, use the congressperson's official title.
4. Outline your concerns in the body of the letter. Share any personal experiences you may have that relate to your concerns. Use information found in this book to strengthen your comments.
5. Request a reply to your letter. This ensures that your letter has been read.
6. Ask your friends and family to write their own letters.

Further Reading

Banerjee, Dillon. *So You Want to Join the Peace Corps: What to Know Before You Go*. Berkeley: Ten Speed Press, 2000.

Espeland, Pamela, and Barbara A. Lewis. *The Kid's Guide to Service Projects: Over 500 Service Ideas for Young People Who Want to Make a Difference*. Minneapolis: Free Spirit Publishing, 1995.

Koob, Jeff. *Two Years in Kingston Town: A Peace Corps Memoir*. Lincoln: Writer's Showcase Press, 2002.

Ogden, Dennis. *Off the Beaten Path*. Philadelphia: Xlibris Corporation, 2001.

Thomsen, Moritz. *Living Poor: A Peace Corps Chronicle*. Seattle: University of Washington Press, 1997.

Web Sites

Peace Corps
www.peacecorps.gov
At the Peace Corps Web site, visitors can access a wealth of information on the Peace Corps. There is a list of countries currently hosting Peace Corps volunteers, as well as a detailed history of the organization.

Peace Corps Kids World
www.peacecorps.gov/kids/index.html
Visitors can find facts about other countries at the Peace Corps Kids World Web site. There are also stories from other cultures and letters from Peace Corps volunteers. One game sends players on a Peace Corps assignment.

Glossary

AIDS: a disease that slowly destroys the body's natural ability to fight off other diseases; stands for Acquired Immune Deficiency Syndrome

at-risk youth: young people who could die or become criminals if they do not receive help

cold war: a battle that is fought with words and threats rather than with guns and bombs

constitution: the basic rules by which the people of a country agree to be governed

developing country: a country that is undergoing economic development

free markets: markets in which each business is allowed to set its own price for its goods and services

landscape architecture: a career dealing with the arrangement of flowers, shrubs, and lawns

latrines: communal toilets

malnutrition: a lack of healthy foods in the diet

pesticides: substances that kill pests such as insects

sterilize: make free from germs and bacteria

underserved community: a community where the needs of the residents are not being met

Index

ACTION 21

Africa 8, 10, 11, 12, 17, 22, 23, 24, 25, 26

AIDS 8, 12, 13, 24, 26

Bush, George W. 23, 24

Caribbean 8, 16, 22

Central America 8, 16, 22, 23, 27

computers 8, 26

Crisis Corps 17, 23, 24, 27

education 5, 10, 11, 16, 18

farming 14, 21

Humphrey, Hubert 5, 20

Kennedy, John F. 4, 5, 6, 7, 20

Pacific 8, 9

Reuss, Henry 5, 20

Shriver, R. Sargent 5, 7, 20

University of Michigan 6, 20

World Wise Schools 18, 22